DISCARDED
Goshen Public Library

GOSHEN PUBLIC LIBRARY
601 SOUTH FIFTH STREET
GOSHEN, IN 46526-3994

DISCARDED
Goshen Public Library

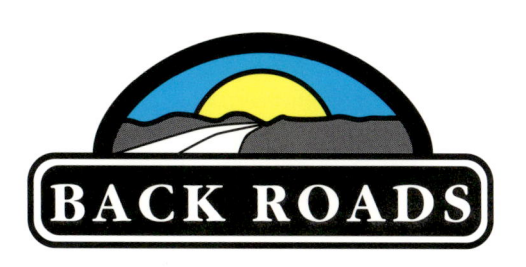

BACK ROADS

OLD NEW ENGLAND

By Lynn M. Stone

THE ROURKE CORPORATION, INC.
Vero Beach, FL 32964

GOSHEN PUBLIC LIBRARY
601 SOUTH FIFTH STREET
GOSHEN, IN 46526-3994

© 1993 The Rourke Corporation, Inc.

All rights reserved. No part of this book may be reproduced or utilized in any form or by any means, electronic or mechanical including photocopying, recording or by any information storage and retrieval system without permission in writing from the publisher.

Edited by Sandra A. Robinson

PHOTO CREDITS

All photos © Lynn M. Stone except page 36 © Vermont Travel Division, page 45 © New Hampshire Office of Travel and Tourist Development, and page 15 courtesy of the United States Department of Agriculture-Forest Service

DEDICATION

For Charlotte, Mel and Melanie, New Englanders all

Library of Congress Cataloging-in-Publication Data
Stone, Lynn M.
    Old New England / by Lynn M. Stone.
        p. cm. — (Back roads)
    Includes index.
    Summary: An introduction to the history, geography, farming, fishing, and tourist sights of New England.
    ISBN 0-86593-303-0
      1. New England—Juvenile literature. [1. New England.] I. Title.
II. Series: Stone, Lynn M. Back roads.
F4.3.S84   1993
974—dc20   93-22881
                                                                           CIP
                                                                             AC

Printed in the USA

TABLE OF CONTENTS

1. Old New England...........4
2. The First New Englanders 12
3. Pastures and Ports 16
4. Lobster Country 26
5. Maple Syrup Country 34
6. Wild Old New England..............37
7. Visiting New England.................42
   Glossary 46
   Index..47

BACK ROADS

CHAPTER 1

OLD NEW ENGLAND

New England's rugged land, its quaint towns, and its historic past make it one of the most enchanting regions in America. Nearly 400 years of American history contribute to the heritage of Connecticut, Rhode Island, Massachusetts, Vermont, New Hampshire and Maine - the six New England states. New England was the first place where English settlers secured a strong footing in the New World, beginning with the arrival of the *Mayflower* in 1620. Later, the 13 English colonies in America tossed off the heavy hand of English rule. The gunfire that began the uprising, which blossomed into the Revolutionary War, first sounded in New England.

New England history still lives in centuries-old buildings, cemeteries, lighthouses, covered bridges, steepled white churches, village inns and old fortresses. Towns throughout the region still have their historic commons, or greens. These broad, grassy plots in town centers were once a gathering place for citizen soldiers, townsfolk and even livestock. Now they are used for arts and crafts fairs.

Sure signs of old New England - rocks, a rushing brook and colorful autumn leaves

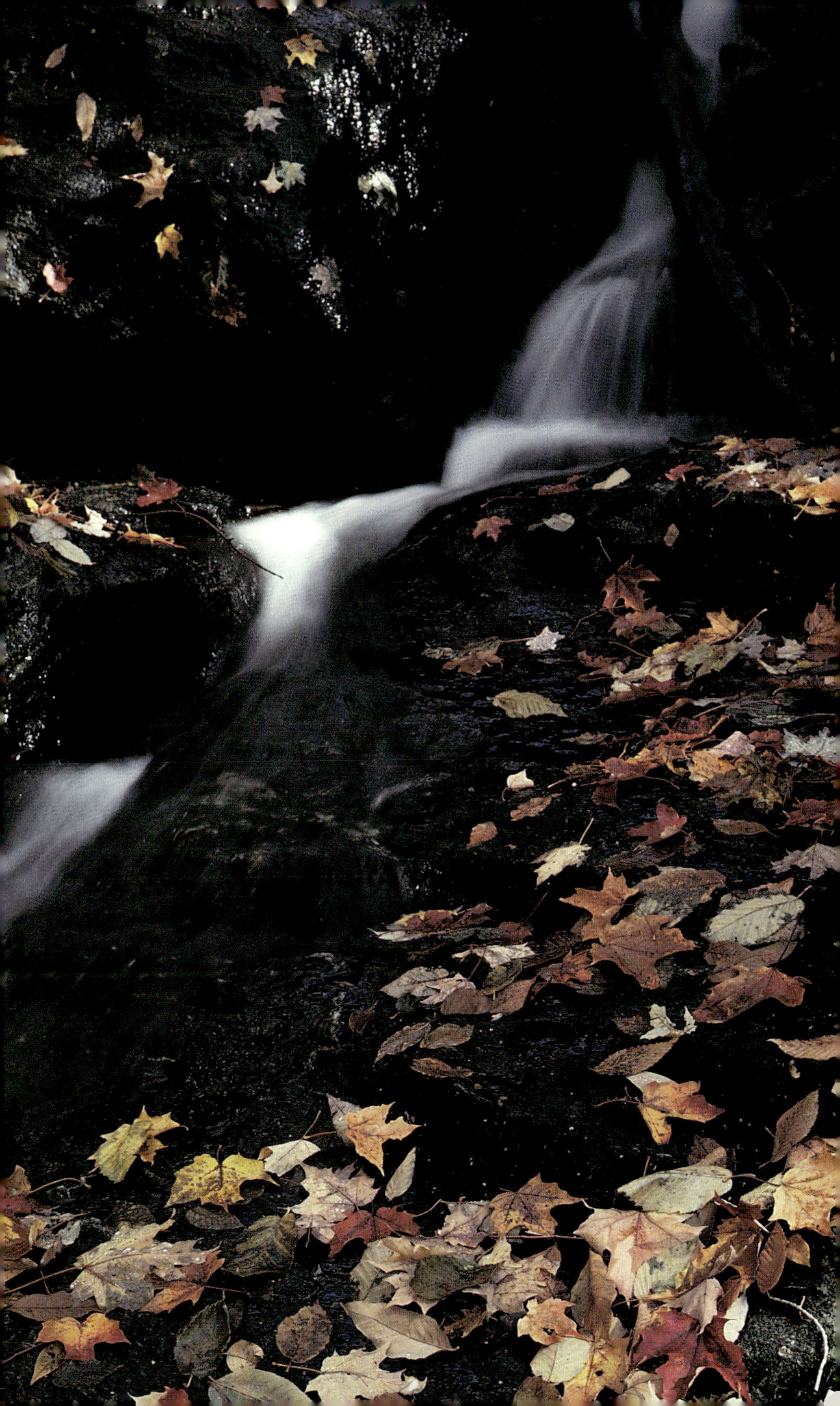

New England's history lives in its old structures, like the Bass Harbor light,

built in 1858 at the entrance of Blue Hill Bay on Maine's Mount Desert Island

Nowhere on earth does autumn arrive with such a splash of color as it does in the woodlands of Vermont and New Hampshire

 The New England countryside, too, bears a reasonable resemblance to its old, historic self. Stone walls constructed hundreds of years ago still mark pasture

boundaries and make hidden stitches in dark woodlands. The brooks and quick rivers still bubble over rocks, tumble down cascades, and knife through ravines. Moose still wade along the lakeshores in Maine. Seals still haul out like great slugs on the sea islands where eiders, gulls, terns and a few Atlantic puffins nest. New Englanders are working hard to put Atlantic salmon back in the Connecticut River. And each fall the New England forest's broad-leaved trees – maples, beeches, birches, oaks and others – are gloriously transformed, as they have always been. The broad-leaved trees trade their green foliage for a few days of splendor in gold, amber, scarlet, orange and purple. Nowhere on earth are the leaves of autumn more vibrant than on the crusty hills and mountains of New Hampshire and Vermont.

New England has several large cities – Boston and Worcester, Massachusetts are the biggest – and all the trappings of modern America. The New England states' economies today are largely based on manufacturing and service industries. Yet along with other **mementoes** of New England's past, several traditional occupations have survived. The ones that draw the most attention are commercial fishing and lobstering, dairy farming, and maple syrup production.

No one who travels in New England is far from a place that retains the flavor of the past. Beyond the next curtain of hills and trees is always another glimpse of an older New England. In this compact region of northeast America, the next curtain of hills is never distant. No point in New England is more than a day's drive from another. In fact, a person can sample all six New England states by car in a single day. That is not recommended, however. Like hot cider, New England should be sipped, not gulped. Just ask a native New Englander.

Morning fog mutes a pocket of vibrant sugar maples in a mixed forest of hardwoods and evergreens in northern New England

New Englanders tend to be rooted to this region. Many of them share the notion that the world more or less starts and finishes somewhere between Connecticut and Maine. They love the changing seasons, the rough-sawn landscape and the ocean. They love the sleepy villages with their lively past and traditional occupations. And New Englanders know that a lifetime isn't long enough to search out the region's enduring charms, much less a day.

CHAPTER 2

THE FIRST NEW ENGLANDERS

Far more than in most regions of the country, New England's historic past is woven into its present. The foundations of modern New England were first kindled in the 1600s, when the tall-masted ships from England began to arrive in the New World. Many of the newcomers were seeking religious and political freedom. Others had a taste for adventure and cheap land. Many found what they were looking for. More often, perhaps, people found incredible hardship. Winters were cruel and food was scarce in the early years. Because the land was heavily forested, farming was delayed until axes could hack clearings. Headstones in New England's ancient cemeteries are testimonials to the risks of life in a new, hard land. The old stones, in a few, weathered words, tell the stories: disease, battles with Native Americans, death at sea.

The most famous early New England settlement was established at Plymouth, Massachusetts, in 1620. Like hundreds of other places in New England, Plymouth borrowed its name from a site in old England. Those borrowed English names rapidly appeared throughout

Behind stone walls, old cemeteries and their nearly forgotten markers reveal some of the hardships faced by early New England settlers

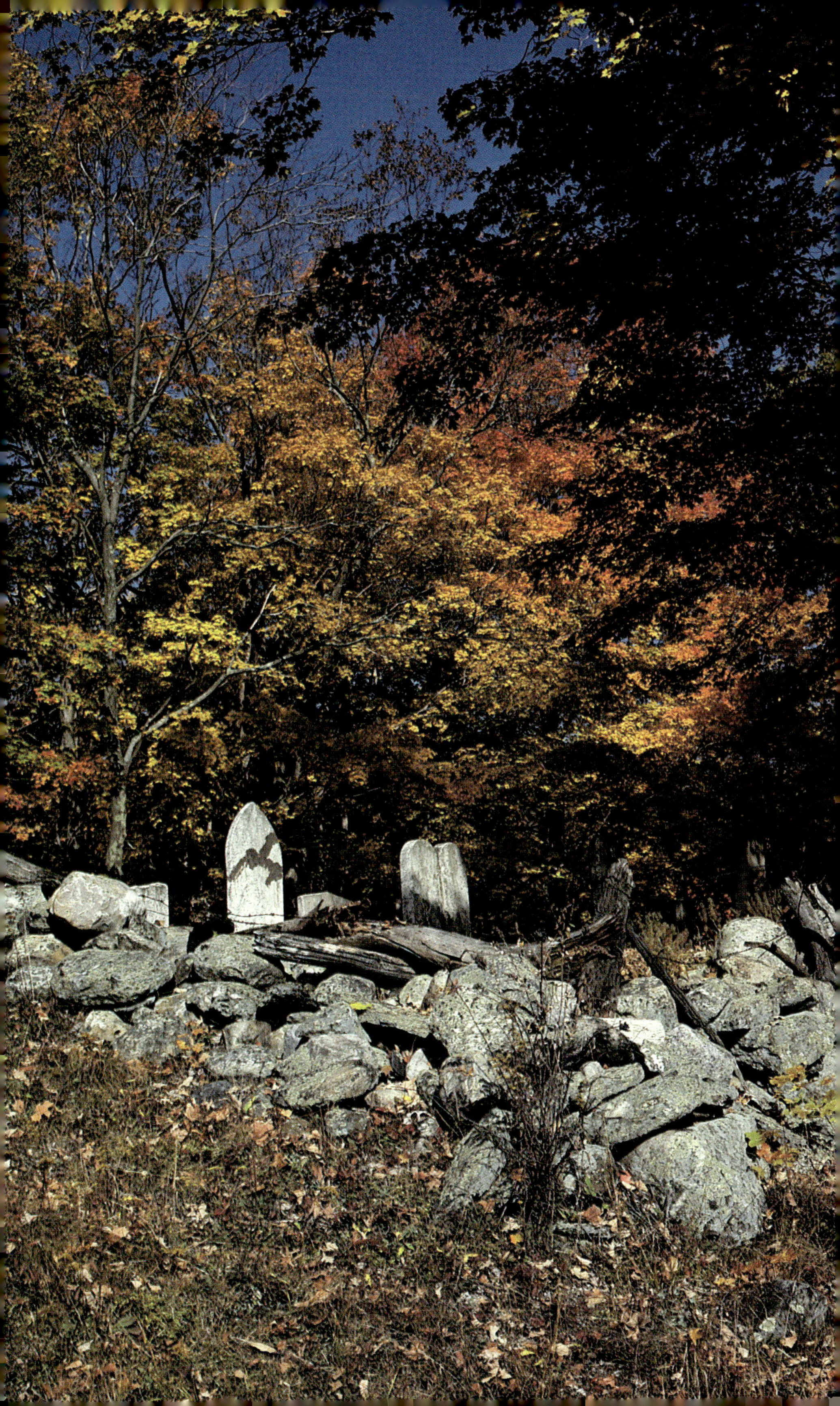

much of New England after 1620. Massachusetts had more than 12,500 European settlers by 1640. Connecticut, Rhode Island, New Hampshire and Maine also had colonies by then. What had begun as a trickle of settlers from England had become a river. While the colonists rejoiced in their growing communities and chopped the forest away, the former landowners grew restless.

The Native Americans in New England were nearly all members of Algonquian tribes, such as the Pequots, Wampanoags and Narragansets. Some of the tribes were quite helpful to the English. Native Americans introduced them to corn, beans, lobsters and other foods. As the number of whites began to build, however, the Native Americans felt increasingly threatened. Their fears were not calmed at all by the settlers' lifestyle. The English had a tremendous appetite for taming the landscape. England itself had long since been reduced to pastures and cities and parks. Now, it seemed, the colonists were intent upon remaking New England in the image of its namesake. They vigorously cleared the forests for villages and farms. They shot more game than necessary and scared away much of what they didn't shoot. Secure in their growing numbers and superior firepower, the settlers continued to help themselves to land and natural resources. The natives began to respond with attacks. The objective was to drive the English into the sea and back to their homeland.

Warfare between the Native Americans and whites became increasingly bloody. In 1637 colonists killed 600 Pequots – men, women and children – near the Mystic River in Connecticut. The defeat of the Pequots ended native resistance in southern New England. Further north and east, fighting continued until 1678. The most

NEW ENGLAND

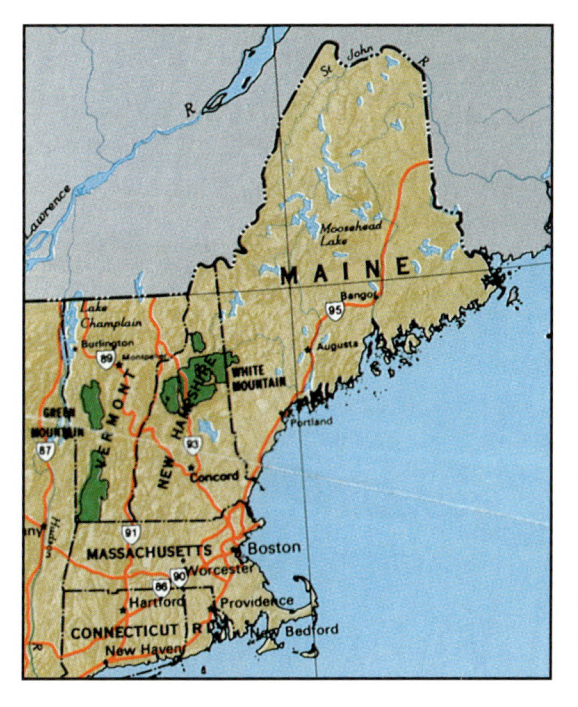

celebrated and defiant of the native leaders was Metacomet, better known as King Philip. In a year of the bloodiest warfare New England has ever experienced, hundreds of colonists died. But Philip was outnumbered and outgunned. He died in battle in 1676. His wife and nine-year-old son were captured by the English and sold as slaves in the West Indies.

The New England colonies remained under British rule for the next 100 years. During the French and Indian Wars (1754-1763), New England colonists and British soldiers fought together against the French and their Native American allies. Yet even before the French and Indian Wars, independent New Englanders had grumbled about the colonies' relations with England. Arguments about taxes, the rights of British soldiers on American soil, and other grievances grew louder. On April 19, 1775, British redcoat soldiers battled colonists at Lexington and Concord, Massachusetts, and along the road to Boston. The American Revolution had begun. It spread quickly throughout the colonies. When it was officially over eight years later, the United States of America emerged – free of British rule.

BACK ROADS

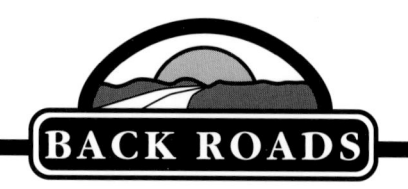

Chapter 3

PASTURES AND PORTS

Long before the union of American colonies forged a new nation, New England settlers established themselves as farmers, commercial fishermen and shipbuilders. The rocky soil resisted farming. The treacherous, storm-tossed Atlantic often resisted sailing ships, too. Nevertheless, the hardy New Englanders – "Yankees" to the British – tamed, if not conquered, both land and sea.

The heydays of Yankee farming, such as they were, vanished long ago. New England rapidly converted from an **agrarian,** or farming, society to a largely industrial one in the early 1800s. New England's port cities and river towns provided a means for export and power. Meanwhile, New England farmers had begun to abandon their farms. The Erie Canal opened an efficient passage between the East and the Midwest. The black soil of the Midwest was much easier to till than the miserably rocky soil of New England, and it was easier to transport crops to New England than to grow them there.

The colonists and later generations of Yankees had cleared tremendous gaps in the great Eastern forest. The settlers were more successful at cutting trees than growing crops, however. Large-scale farming in New England was not meant to be. The colossal, frozen rivers of ice called glaciers had seen to that many thousands of

The pastures that colonial farmers toiled to clear have regrown into the woodlands that Native Americans loved

years beforehand. The glaciers bulldozed soil away, exposing rock. They also left calling cards – glacial garbage in the form of more rocks. New Englanders will still tell you that their fields grow stones. As the ground freezes each winter, the frost action splits the ground and causes upheavals, pushing stones upward.

As the New Englanders cleared trees to open pasture, they also cleared the stones. They piled them on wooden sleds, or **sledges,** pulled by **oxen.** These hard-working cattle were stronger than horses and could live on a lighter diet. Farmers piled rocks from the sledges into stone walls. The walls separated farms, and many of them

The New Englanders' passion for pastures, at the expense of forest, was one of many points of friction between the English colonists and Native Americans

were built high enough to contain goats, sheep and other livestock. Thousands of miles of stone walls still thread the New England countryside. The walls are not particularly functional anymore, but New Englanders have generally chosen to keep them rather than cart them away. Building a stone wall is laborious. Taking one apart is not much easier.

It is not uncommon to find stone walls in woodlands. Forests have gradually reclaimed the old farms and their stone boundaries. Connecticut and Vermont, for example, had lost 75 percent of their forests by the mid-19th century. Now these states are 75 percent forest! In Maine and New Hampshire, forests have returned to about 85 percent of their former acreage. More of New England is forested today than it was during George Washington's presidency late in the 1700s!

New England has a few farms today. Many of them raise shrubs and other **ornamental** plants. There are also cranberry farms in Massachusetts, tobacco farms in Connecticut, and potato farms in northern Maine. One of the surviving traditional farms is the family-operated dairy. Dairy farms are in all of the New England states, but Vermont is the center of New England dairy production. It has about 165,000 dairy cattle, more than the other five New England states combined. Vermont ranks 15th in the nation as a milk-producing state.

Along the New England coast another traditional occupation has survived. Whaling is gone, but in towns like Gloucester, Chatham, New Bedford and Provincetown, Massachusetts, commercial fishing boats still tie up at the docks. These little **fleets** of boats fish the offshore waters of the New England coast. Many of them drag huge nets called **trawls.** They catch cod, herring, flounder, hake, pollock, ocean perch and other species of fish.

The Massachusetts fish catch, including its harvest of **shellfish** such as lobsters, is worth about $260 million annually. Massachusetts has the seventh most valuable fish harvest of the 50 states. New Bedford's yearly haul of fish is the most valuable of any one port in the United States.

Harvest of the sea, bluefish sprawl on a fisherman's dockside table in Massachusetts

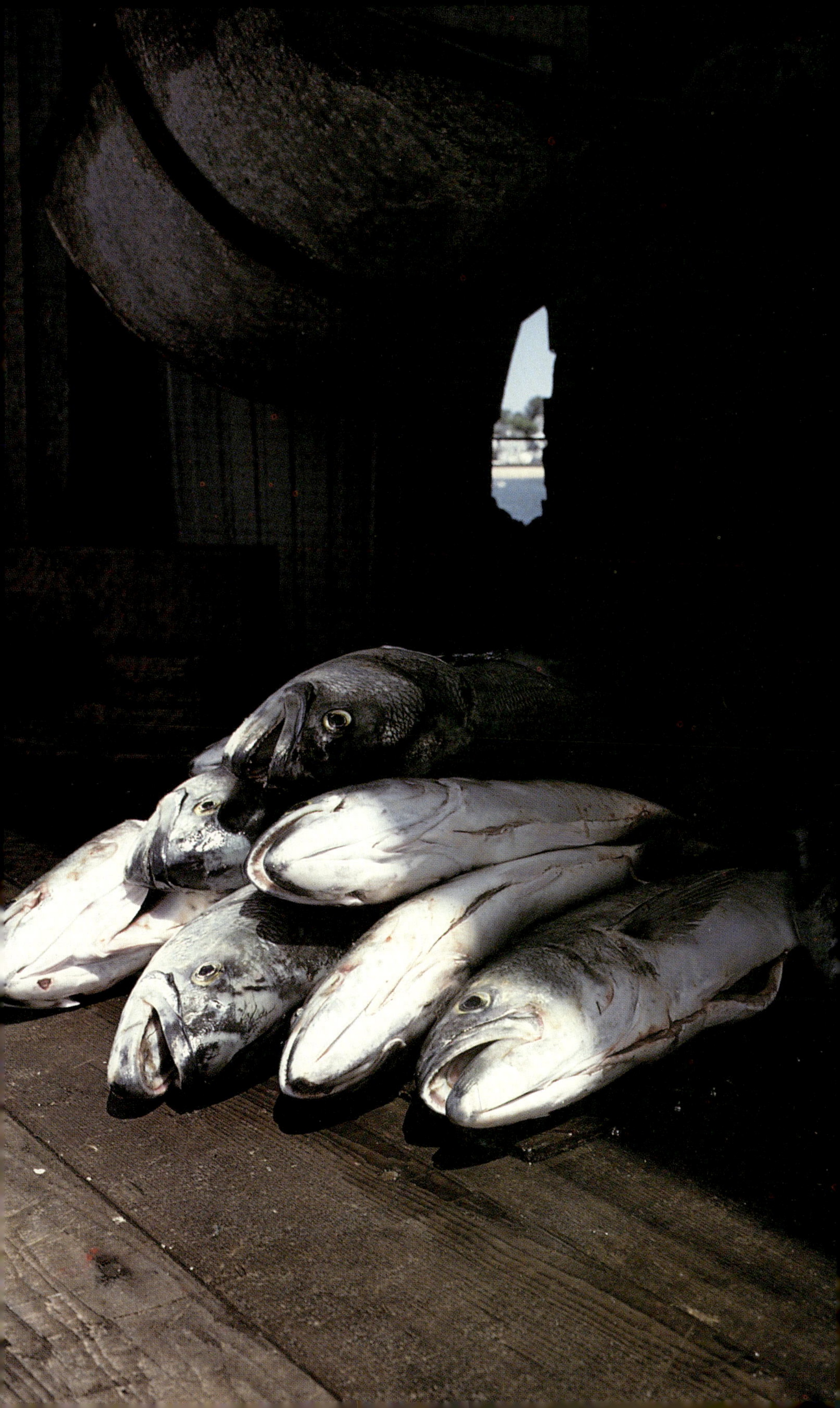

A traditional, family-owned dairy farm in Connecticut, where dairies have become scarce

    In the old days, New England fishermen often worked their nets from small wooden boats – dories – that were dispatched from a larger, "mother" ship. For men adrift in the dories, the possibility of fog was an ever-present danger. Men in dories could be overtaken by fog and lose contact with the big ship. Between storms and fog, many men perished at sea. Towns like Gloucester had far too many widows, and there was truth in the saying that the history of the Gloucester fishermen was written in tears.

Ocean fishing isn't as hazardous today in the age of electronics and gasoline engines. It is still hard labor, however, and New England sailors still risk the mood swings of the Atlantic.

This chest-high stone wall weaves through woodland that was once Vermont farmland

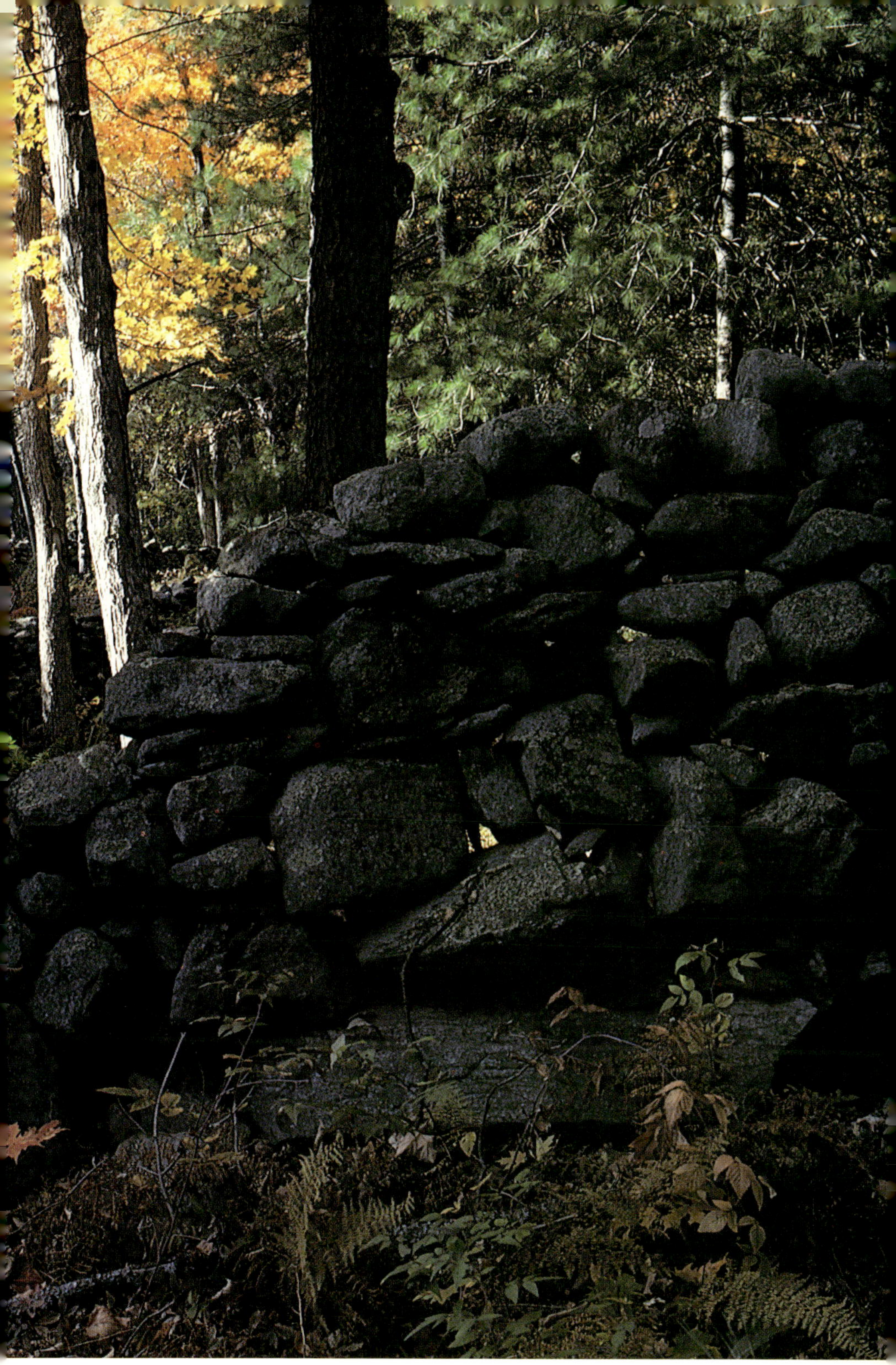

BACK ROADS

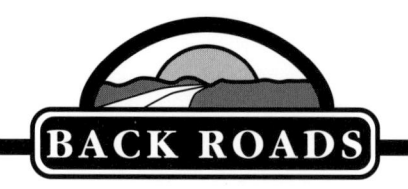

Chapter 4

LOBSTER COUNTRY

None of the traditional occupations in old New England is more colorful than the lobster industry, which is as much part of the Maine coast as the rocks and sea fogs.

To a scientist, the American lobster is a **crustacean,** a hard-shelled creature with a jointed body, no bones and little brainpower. To most people, the tasty lobster is a meal, a treat for a king's table. Found in the cold Atlantic waters off New England and the Canadian seaside provinces, lobsters may weigh up to 20 pounds. More typically, lobsters weigh a pound or two and fit very nicely on a plate.

Lobsters live in the coastal waters of Maine. The demand for lobster meat, most of which is in the animal's tail and two large claws, created an industry long ago. Maine's Native Americans introduced lobster to the European settlers some 300 years ago. The lobster has been a favorite of seafood lovers ever since. Live lobsters are greenish-black, but their shells turn bright red as they are cooked.

Lobster harvesters catch their quarry much as they have for generations. A lobsterman baits a wooden or steel trap called a lobster pot with fish. Each trap is

Gulls mob a fishing boat working in the Gulf of Maine

weighted so that it will anchor itself on the ocean bottom. A cord with a brightly colored float is attached to the trap. The float marks the trap's location. It also keeps one end of the cord at the ocean surface so that the lobsterman can retrieve the trap.

    A lobster pot resembles an orange crate with netting at the ends. The netting permits a hungry lobster to enter the pot, but not exit. A day or two after baiting traps, the lobsterman hauls them up and *carefully* removes any lobsters. The animal's big front claws can inflict a nasty cut. The lobsterman either binds the claws or inserts wooden plugs into the claw joints to "tame" the lobster.

Lobster boats, owned largely by people whose ancestors were also lobster fishermen, rock gently on a high tide

    A lobsterman may operate from 300 to 1,500 traps. If each of the pots averages a pound of lobster, the lobsterman is content. In Maine the annual lobster catch totals several million pounds, more than in any other state.

    Lobster boats are distinctive craft about 35 feet long. A lobster boat has a high, sharp **bow** and a small, stair-shaped cabin. The boat is built to slice neatly through waves, yet roll with the ocean swells. Lobster boats are not particularly fast, but they are ruggedly seaworthy. Continuing another

New England tradition, Maine has several shipbuilders. Nearly all of Maine's lobster boats were built in-state.

Depending upon the season, a lobster boat may work close to shore or cruise 20 miles into the choppy Atlantic. Lobsters usually enter shallow water in warm months, then retreat to deeper water in November.

Maine's coastal lobster country is New England at its best – rustic, weathered, wrapped in the traditions of the sea. The tang of salt and lobster pots braces the air.

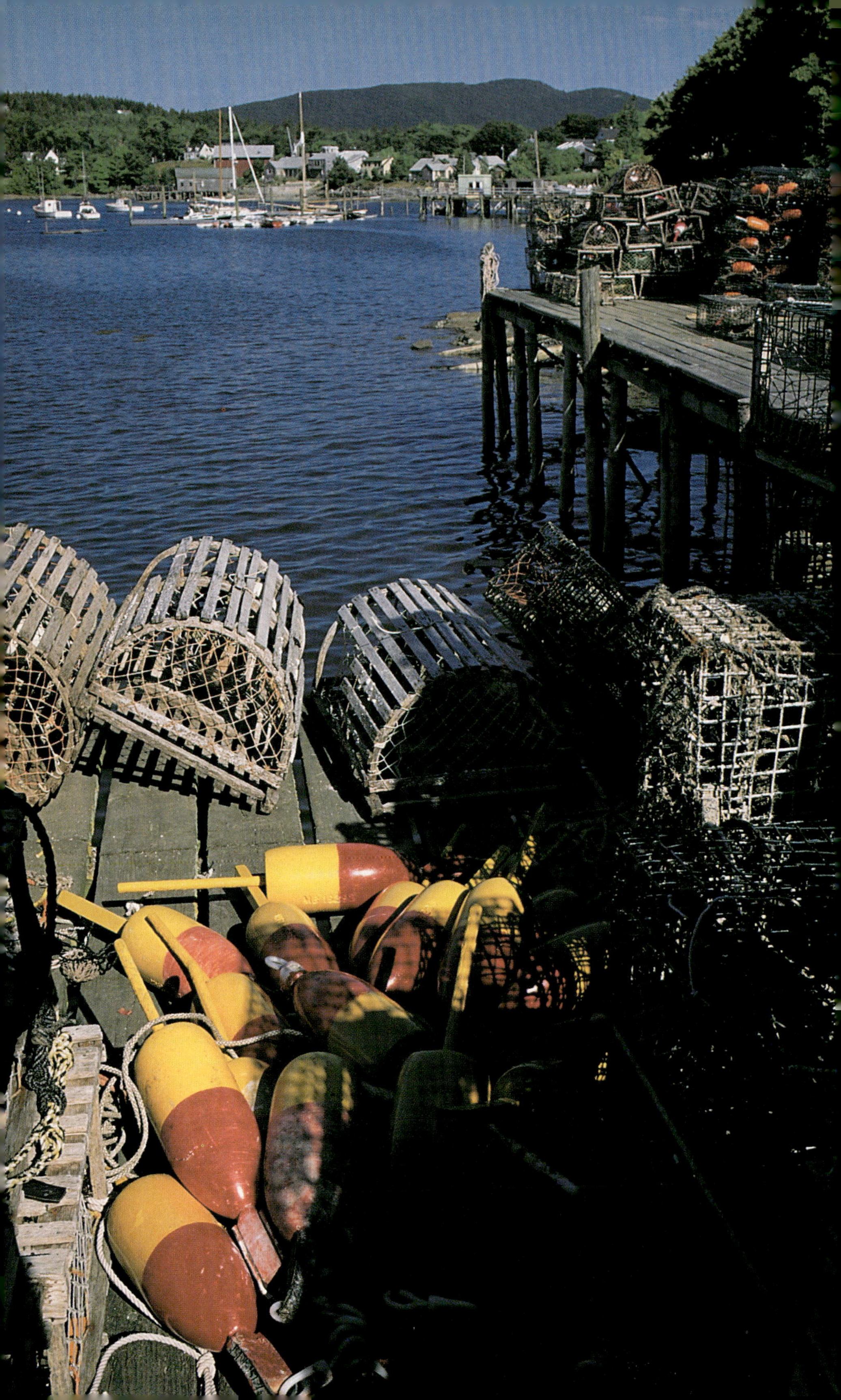

Summer fogs steal into Down East lobster ports

Foghorns bleat solemn warnings to ships when sea lanes are swallowed by fog. At Wiscasset, the hulks of two turn-of-the-century sailing ships, the *Luther Little* and *Hesper,* lie **moldering** in the bay like beached whales. Scattered along the coast, old lighthouses wink at passing ships. The Pemaquid Light has been a sentinel on the rocks since 1827. Lobster boats bob in the sheltered inlets of Port Clyde, Sunshine, Jonesport, Southwest Harbor, Camden, Stonington and scores of other towns. Modest wooden homes and mighty estates stand along the shores and on forested hills above the harbors. Old **wharves,** stacked high with lobster pots and littered with snarls of line and floats, step on wooden stilts into the harbors of towns all along the Maine coast.

Lobster floats and traps on a dock in historic Southwest Harbor, Maine, where in 1613 the British warship Treasurer *attacked a French settlement that was the first white settlement on Mount Desert Island*

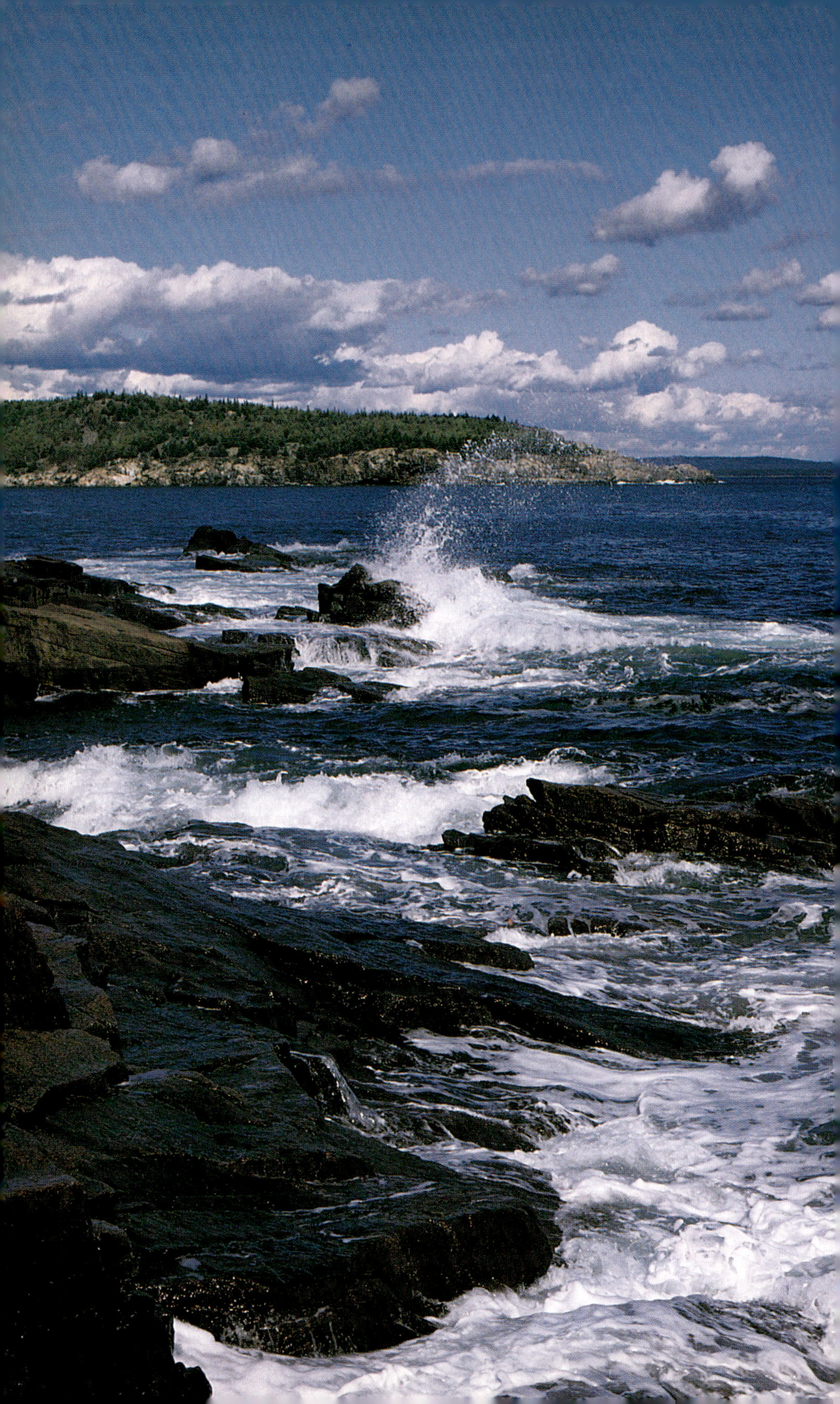

It is a remarkable coast. In a bald eagle's straight line of flight the Maine coast is 228 miles long. But the coast is jagged, as if it has been ripped from the sea. If someone followed the shoreline of each finger of land and islet, that person would hike nearly 3,500 miles from one end of the Maine coast to the other.

This is "Down East," as New Englanders call Maine and its coast. The term was coined by **mariners** from Boston in an era when men still went to sea in tall-masted ships. Bound for Maine and the Canadian **maritime** ports, the prevailing winds pushed ships *down*wind and *east*. The great fleet of commercial sailing ships is gone, but some of the Down East Maine that the old sea captains knew lingers.

Maine's remarkable coast - 3,500 miles of shore bathed and battered by the sea

Chapter 5
MAPLE SYRUP COUNTRY

Each fall the leaves of Vermont sugar maples blaze red. The trees enthrall thousands of "leafers," people who tour northern New England to witness the magnificent fall colors.

Although prized for autumn foliage, sugar maples are also valued for their wood and sap, a watery liquid that courses through the tree. Maple syrup and maple sugar are made from sugar maple sap. Among all the states, Vermont is the largest producer of maple syrup. Three other New England states – Massachusetts, New Hampshire and Connecticut – market much smaller quantities of maple syrup.

Vermonters have gathered pails of maple sap since the early days of settlement. Vermonters processed most of the sap for maple sugar back then. Sugar was more important than syrup, and maple sap was the main source of sugar. That changed in the late 1800s when the cane sugar we use today became available in large and inexpensive quantities.

Another of New England's traditional activities, the maple syrup process begins in late winter. Mild days of late winter turn into chilly nights. The daily extremes in air temperature start the sap flowing, and a harvest begins. Even in their leafless grays and browns, sugar maples are special trees.

A Vermonter collects maple sap in the traditional way

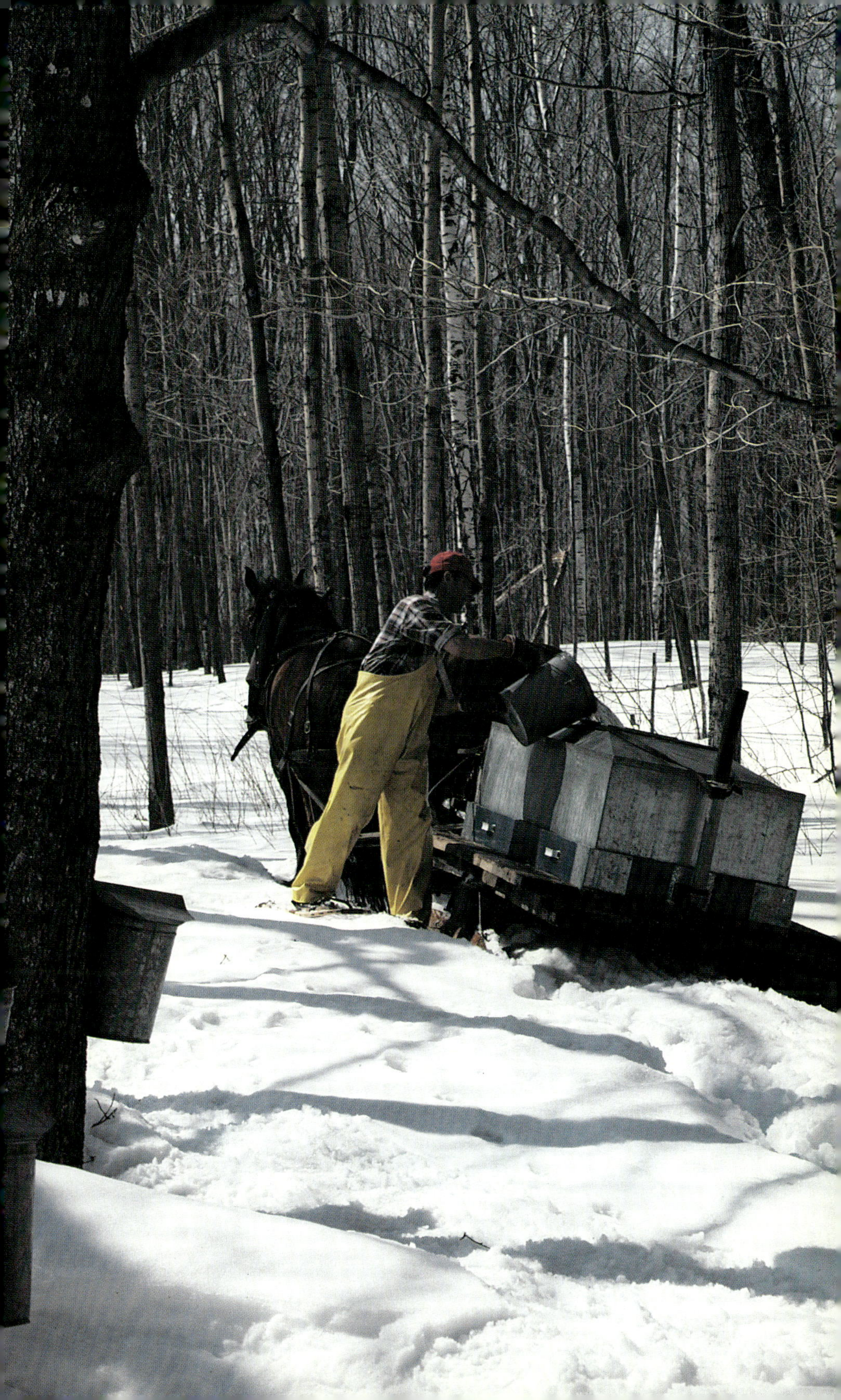

A Vermont sugarhouse in October, when the maples draw crowds of "leafers"

A sap collector drills a hole in the sugar maple tree and inserts a spout. The flow of sap drips from the spout into a bucket. The buckets are collected and taken to a small, wooden sugarhouse. A more modern method directs the sap through plastic lines that lead directly to the sugarhouse.

Maple sap doesn't look like deep-golden maple syrup. Sap is colorless and runs like water. But a strange thing occurs in the creaky old sugarhouses – with the proper know-how, watery sap will become sweet maple syrup.

Sap is placed in a pan and heated by a wood-fueled fire. The water in the sap begins to **evaporate;** it rises as steam. While the heat boils some of the water away, the natural solids in the sap – salts, sugars and acids – remain as syrup. About 40 gallons of sap produce one gallon of maple syrup. If the sap is boiled for a longer period, it yields maple sugar.

BACK ROADS

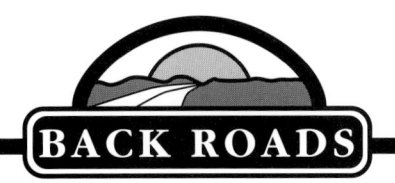

Chapter 6
WILD OLD NEW ENGLAND

New England has been farmed, logged and industrialized. Nevertheless, it has stubbornly held on to many of its natural treasures. New England has a wild side.

In some parts of New England, the rocky ground and windblown ridges have kept human activities at a distance. More important is the fact that northern New England's population growth has been slow. That has been helpful in curbing misuse of land. New Hampshire, Vermont and Maine have fewer than 3 million residents. In addition, New Englanders of recent generations have a tradition of caring for their land.

Forest once covered almost every dry acre of New England. Forest is still the dominant feature of the landscape. Most of the forest is **second-growth** – trees that grew after an older forest was cut. Many of the second-growth forests are more than 150 years old. Here and there are still older groves where white pines, hemlocks or maples tower in stands that have never been cut.

Most of the large tracts of wild forest lands are in the mountains – the Berkshires and Taconics of Connecticut and Massachusetts, the Green Mountains of Vermont, and the White Mountains of New Hampshire and southwestern

The wild ranges of Cadillac Mountain in Acadia National Park look down upon the sea islands and coves of Frenchman Bay

Maine. Wild forests are also spread throughout Maine, a state that is nearly 90 percent wooded.

Forests are not the only wild lands. New England has dozens of clear lakes ringed by rocks and woods. Some of the most fascinating of the wild lands are **bogs.** Bogs are old ponds and lakes that have begun to choke on their own vegetation. As the plants die, they accumulate and gradually fill in the lake basin. Meanwhile, a spongy mattress of plants spreads across the surface of the dying lake. New England is rich in bogs, hillside wetlands called **fens,** and swamps where thickets of wild blueberries grow.

Several of New England's outstanding wild lands are publicly owned. The National Park Service is the guardian of Acadia National Park, New England's only national park. Acadia includes much of rugged Mount Desert Island and other coastal properties in Maine. Acadia is a

Burnham Brook, in the first flush of fall, lashes through a Nature Conservancy preserve in Connecticut

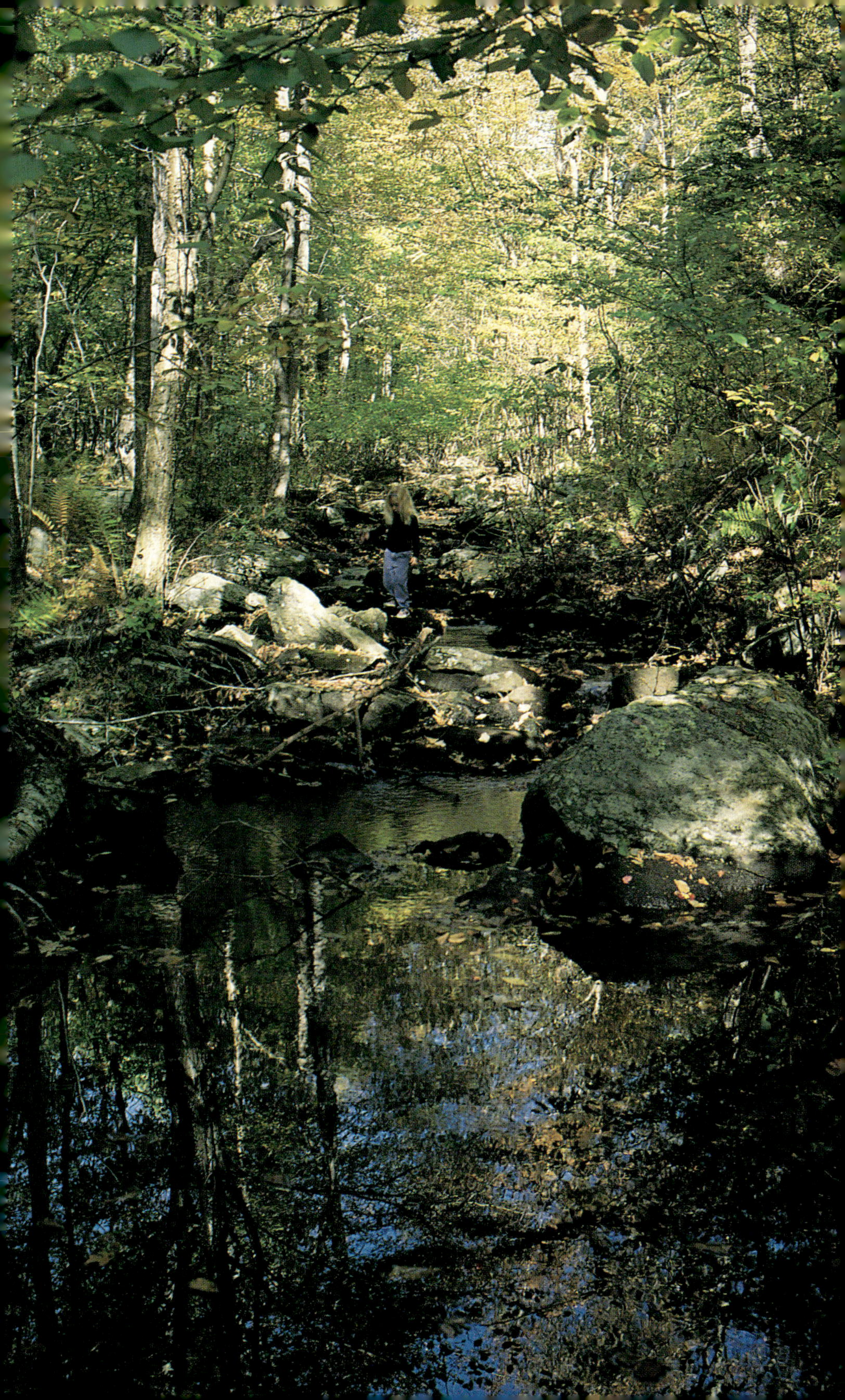

Cape Cod National Seashore is the setting for this salt meadow and marsh, a rich nursery for wildlife

spectacular region where the rocky shore meets the surging Atlantic. Several lakes, ponds and bogs are in the park below 1,530-foot Cadillac Mountain, the highest point on the Atlantic seaboard between Canada and Brazil. Cape Cod National Seashore in Massachusetts is also part of the national park system. The national seashore preserves long stretches of beach and dune, and pockets of salt marsh, swamp and woodland.

    The U.S. Forest Service manages the White Mountain National Forest in New Hampshire and Green Mountain National Forest in Vermont. The highest peaks in New England, climaxed by windswept Mount Washington at 6,288 feet above sea level, are in the Presidential Range of the White Mountains. The U.S. Fish and Wildlife Service operates Monomoy National Wildlife Refuge, which includes island beach strands in the Atlantic just beyond Cape Cod, and wonderfully wild Moosehorn National

Wildlife Refuge in Maine. The federal government also helps sponsor the 703 miles of Appalachian Trail that wind through the high country of Connecticut, Massachusetts, New Hampshire, Vermont and Maine.

Among the hundreds of state parks and forests in New England, Baxter State Park in Maine is a delightful example. Baxter is a 200,000-acre wilderness of peaks, lakes, evergreen forests and 5,268-foot Mount Katahdin. Moose live here along with porcupines, river otters, beavers, loons, lynxes and bald eagles.

Probably no single private organization has been more helpful in protecting wild lands in New England than the Nature Conservancy. It has purchased dozens of extraordinary parcels of land for the protection of animals, plants and natural beauty.

A great hands-on adventure in coastal New England is digging for clams, as this man is doing in the mud of Monomoy Island

BACK ROADS

CHAPTER 7

VISITING NEW ENGLAND

You can experience New England in several different ways. One way is to leisurely drive or bicycle the climbing, dipping, winding back roads. Getting lost can be half the fun!

Visit the places where the traditions of old New England are still part of everyday life – a lobster wharf in Maine, or a sugarhouse on a Vermont farm. Find a dairy farm with its pastures marked by stone walls. Visit a country store and stay in an old inn where people have been finding a night's rest for 200 years.

An artist paints the Provincetown, Massachusetts, waterfront, guarded by the Pilgrim Monument that honors the arrival of pilgrims here in 1620

Bed and breakfasts and old inns welcome New England's back road travelers now, as they have for more than 300 years

    Visit the many historic places and the living history museums. Boston National Historic Park is a feast for history lovers. It includes several of the buildings and sites from the opening days of the American Revolution against the British. Here a visitor will find Bunker Hill, where in June, 1775, the bloodiest battle of the entire Revolutionary War occurred. Nearby Minute Man National Historic Park preserves Revolutionary War battlegrounds and several historic homes.

    At New England's living history museums, costumed interpreters and re-created buildings bring the past to the present. Strawberry Banke is a restored colonial seaport in Portsmouth, New Hampshire. Mystic Seaport re-creates an old port in Mystic, Connecticut. Plimoth Plantation re-creates the town of Plimoth, Massachusetts, as it was in 1627 – long before it was spelled "Plymouth." Old Sturbridge Village, also in Massachusetts, demonstrates how pioneers lived in a rural New England village of the early 1800s.

Many of New England's sons and daughters are remembered in historic sites, homes and museums. The homes of 19th-century writers Nathaniel Hawthorne *(The House of Seven Gables)* and Louisa May Alcott *(Little Women)* are in Minute Man National Historic Park. One of America's finest 20th-century poets, Robert Frost, is remembered with the Robert Frost National Recreation Trail near Middlebury, Vermont. Revolutionary War General Nathanael Green's homestead is in Coventry, Rhode Island. One of many New England museums showing regional art is the Farnsworth Library and Art Museum in Rockland, Maine. It exhibits work by Boston-born Winslow Homer, famous for his 19th-century portrayals of **seafarers.** The work of a modern artist, Andrew Wyeth, noted for his scenes of rural Maine, is also featured at the museum. New England remains a favorite haunt for artists captivated by the region's blend of cultural and natural beauty. Provincetown, at the tip of Cape Cod, and Monhegan Island, Maine, have an abundance of artists in summer residence.

Outdoorsy types will find limitless outlets for their energy and sense of adventure in New England. Hike a forest trail. (Beware of ruffed grouse, or partridge, though. These woodland relatives of quail and pheasants will flush under a hiker's nose and leave him shaken with fright.) Or take the spectacular journey to the top of Mount Washington. The summit can be reached by a winding, eight-mile auto road, by cog railway or by one of several hiking trails.

Traveling from the bottom to the top of Mount Washington is nearly as eye-popping as Jack's trip up the beanstalk. The journey begins in a maple and birch forest at the base. As the altitude increases, these trees yield to

Mount Washington's summit looms above the autumn foliage in New Hampshire's Presidential Range

cold-hardy spruce and balsam fir. Higher still, the evergreens thin out and disappear. On the rocky mountain summit, above **timberline,** only shrubs and tundra plants – like those of Greenland and Alaska – can survive. The wind and bitter cold of this mountain are legendary. A weather station atop Mount Washington recorded 231-mile per hour gales on April 12, 1934. They were the strongest winds ever measured on land.

　　Weather aside, the view of the surrounding peaks in the Presidential Range (part of the Appalachian chain) and the countryside below are breathtaking. Of course, viewing days are fairly rare. Mount Washington often has its head in the clouds, and snow may fall on the summit in any month.

　　The story is told that P.T. Barnum, of circus fame, prowled the summit of Mount Washington on a clear day early in the 20th century. Mr. Barnum, who advertised his circus as "The Greatest Show on Earth," was inclined to exaggerate. But his description of the New England countryside below and beyond Mount Washington that day may have been just barely shy of the truth. It was, he said, "The Second Greatest Show on Earth."

Glossary

agrarian - relating to the farmer's way of life; agricultural

bog - a type of natural wetland that is a pond or lake filled with its own decaying vegetation

bow - the forward part of a boat or ship

crustacean - a family of hard-shelled, boneless animals including shrimps, crabs, lobsters and others

evaporate - to change into vapor or steam

fen - a type of natural wetland often found on hillsides

fleet - a group of boats or ships of similar size and purpose

mariner - a seaman or sailor

maritime - having to do with the sea, such as a maritime province of Canada

memento - souvenir

moldering - decaying

ornamental - decorative; used as an ornament

oxen - male cattle raised for labor, such as hauling

seafarers - those who sail the sea

second-growth - a forest that grows in place of one that has been destroyed

shellfish - any of several edible, hard-shelled creatures of the sea, such as lobsters, scallops, clams and oysters

sledge - a sledlike device with runners, used for transporting loads

timberline - the place above which no trees can grow because of the cold, wind, and poor-quality or frozen soil

trawl - a large net that is dragged along the sea bottom

wharf - a structure extending from shore into a harbor, which boats and ships lie alongside and gather or discharge cargo

INDEX

Acadia National Park 38
Alcott, Louisa May 44
Algonquian tribes 14
American Revolution (see
  Revolutionary War)
animals 41
Appalachian Trail 41
artists 44
Atlantic Ocean 16, 23, 29, 40
autumn 10, 34
Barnum, P.T. 45
Baxter State Park 41
Berkshire Mountains 37
blueberries 38
bogs 38, 40
Boston, MA 10, 15, 33
Boston National Historic Park 43
British soldiers 15
brooks 9
Bunker Hill 43
Cadillac Mountain 40
Camden, ME 31
Cape Cod 40, 44
Cape Cod National Seashore 40
cemeteries 12
Chatham, MA 20
churches 4
colonies 4, 15, 16
colonists 14, 15, 16
commons 4
Concord, MA 15
Connecticut 4, 11, 14, 19, 20, 34, 37, 41
Connecticut River 10
corn 14
Coventry, RI 44
crafts fairs 4
cranberry farms 20
crops 16
dairy farm 42
dairy farming 10
disease 12
dories 22
Down East (Maine) 33
East 16

eiders 10
England 12, 14, 15
English colonies (see *colonies*)
English settlers 4
Erie Canal 16
fall (see *autumn*)
farmers 16
farming 16
farms 14, 16, 17, 19, 20
Farnsworth Library and Art Museum 44
fens 38
fish 20
fishermen 16, 22, 23
fishing 10, 23
fishing boats 20
fog 22, 26, 31
foghorns 31
forests 14, 16, 19, 37, 38, 44
French (soldiers) 15
French and Indian Wars 15
Frost, Robert 44
glaciers 16, 17
Gloucester, MA 20, 23
Green Mountain National Forest 40
Green Mountains 37
Green, Nathanael 44
gulls 10
Hawthorne, Nathaniel 44
Hesper 31
Homer, Winslow 44
horses 17
inns 4, 42
Jonesport, ME 31
King Philip (see *Metacomet*)
lakes 38, 40
"leafers" 34
Lexington, MA 15
lighthouses 4, 31
lobster boat 28, 29, 31
lobstering 10
lobsterman 27, 28
lobster pot 26, 27, 28, 29, 31
lobsters 14, 20, 26, 27, 29
Luther Little 31

47

Index

Maine 4, 10, 11, 14, 20, 26, 28, 29, 31, 33, 37, 38, 41, 42, 44
Maine coast 26, 31, 33
maple sap 34, 36
maple sugar 34, 36
maples (see *sugar maples*)
maple syrup 10, 34, 36
Massachusetts 4, 14, 20, 34, 37, 40, 41, 43
Mayflower 4
Metacomet 15
Middlebury, VT 44
Midwest 16
Minute Man National Historic Park 43, 44
Monhegan Island, ME 44
Monomoy National Wildlife Refuge 40
moose 9, 41
Moosehorn National Wildlife Refuge 40, 41
Mount Desert Island, ME 38
Mount Katahdin 41
Mount Washington 40, 44, 45
museums 44
Mystic, CT 43
Mystic River 14
Mystic Seaport 43
Narragansets 14
Native Americans 12, 14, 15, 26
Nature Conservancy 41
New Bedford, MA 20
New Englanders 10, 11, 15, 16, 17, 18, 33, 37
New Hampshire 4, 10, 20, 34, 37, 40, 41
Old Sturbridge Village 43
oxen 17
pastures 17, 42
Pemaquid Light 31
Pequots 14
plants 41
Plimoth Plantation 43
Plymouth, MA 12, 43
Port Clyde, ME 31
Portsmouth, NH 43
potato farms 20

Presidential Range 40, 45
Provincetown, MA 20, 44
puffins 10
ravines 9
Revolutionary War 4, 15, 43
Rhode Island 4, 14
rivers 9
Robert Frost National Recreation Trail 44
Rockland, ME 44
rocks 16, 17, 26, 38
salmon, Atlantic 10
seals 10
seasons 11
second-growth (forest) 37
shellfish 20
shipbuilders 16, 29
ships 16, 33
sleds 17
soil 16, 17
Southwest Harbor, ME 31
stone walls 8, 18, 19, 42
Stonington, ME 31
Strawberry Banke 43
sugarhouse 36, 42
sugar maples 34, 36
Sunshine, ME 31
swamps 38
Taconic Mountains 37
terns 10
tobacco farms 20
trawls 20
trees 10, 16, 17, 34
Vermont 4, 10, 19, 34, 37, 40, 41
Vermonters 34
villages 11
Wampanoags 14
wharves 31
White Mountain National Forest 40
White Mountains 37, 40
wild lands 38, 41
winter 12, 17, 34
Wiscasset, ME 31
Worcester, MA 10
Wyeth, Andrew 44
Yankees 16

GOSHEN PUBLIC LIBRARY
601 SOUTH FIFTH STREET
GOSHEN, IN 46526-3994